Knowing The Score

The A-B-C's Of Rating Realty Customers

Knowing The Score

The A-B-C's Of Rating Realty Customers

Steve Hoffacker

CAPS, MCSP, MIRM

Knowing The Score

The A-B-C's Of Rating Realty Customers

Cover photo by Steve Hoffacker.

West Palm Beach, Florida, USA

ISBN: 978-0-9843524-1-8

Each real estate customer — whether a buyer or seller — has different needs and requirements. Some are able to make decisions quickly while others need weeks — or even months or years — to make a decision. Some will never make a decision. Devoting the same amount of time or energy to working with each customer is not a wise or productive use of your resources. Knowing who to focus on and work with is the key.

Table Of Contents

Chapter *Page*

Preface

I appreciate that you bought this book and that you are reading it.

It shows that you are a professional and that you are interested in being an even better real estate agent than you are right now – whether you are doing listings, sales, or both.

This book is going to revolutionize the way you work with your customers – and how you make sales.

It's going to energize you and give you a fresh perspective on managing and allocating your time and deciding how to work with your customer base.

It will empower you to use your resources more effectively and efficiently.

You'll be able to be much more strategic in how you conduct your initial presentations, subsequent contacts, and return appointments.

We know that the sales process begins when a customer contacts you by phone or email or when they visit your office, open house, or sales center.

Not all clients and customers are created the same, however.

They differ in terms of their interest level, needs, requirements, capacity to like or want what you're offering or what you have to show them, and their ability to make a decision — as well as how quickly any decision is likely to happen.

Some customers will just be curious or "just looking" when they visit you.

Others will need to make a decision immediately.

Some people will have a very hard time imagining themselves living in the home you're showing them because of their needs or requirements.

A few will show no interest at all in what you have, and you'll wonder why they even came or contacted you.

How then do you decide which people are the most serious while you're working with them?

Who should be re-contacted right away, and who may not need any immediate consideration?

Who needs additional attention after they leave your sales center, open house, or office — and which ones require very little or no contact?

In this book, I offer specific ways for you to determine which customers are the most deserving of your time and attention and which customers are likely not to purchase anything from you — no matter what you do.

The latter will not require much, if any, of your time after you initially meet with them.

This way you'll know which ones to focus on and how to manage your time and resources quite well.

The basis for this efficiency is an effective rating system that determines and ascertains each customer's ability and willingness to make a decision and prioritizes them accordingly.

This system focuses on using the decision date as the key indicator.

The move-in or closing date is less important.

In terms of rating customers and determining which ones to work with, the decision date is what counts — for either a purchase (buyer) or listing (seller).

Obviously, those who are able to make a decision the quickest are your best opportunities for a sale or listing and the ones you'll want to concentrate on first, but there is a little more to it than just focusing on these people.

In this book, I will reveal and explain the best, most effective grading system for all of your traffic. No other rating system is necessary.

Every single person or customer unit who contacts or visits you, regardless of their level of interest in listing their existing home or acquiring another home — or in obtaining it with you — can be accommodated by this system.

As a result of reading this book and implementing my system, you will be a much more efficient and productive real estate salesperson.

You'll be able to prioritize your customers and determine appropriate courses of action based on their ability to make a decision.

Knowing The Score

The A-B-C's Of Rating Realty Customers

1

Why You Need A Rating System

Everyone Has Their Own Agenda

People are different, and they shop for homes or look for someone to help them in various ways.

Some of the people who contact you, want to meet with you, want you to help them find their next home, or want you to market their current one, will have more immediate needs than others.

Some will have almost no interest in acting at all, and you'll question their motives for even contacting you.

People differ in terms of how well they might like what you are offering or what you intend to show them – also in their apparent willingness, ability, timing, or desire toward making a decision.

Just from initial impressions, it may not be that easy to tell which of your customers or leads are interested in working with you and those who are not.

More than one meeting or conversation may be necessary before you determine how serious someone is.

Because people have different needs, interest levels, and timing for making their decisions, giving everyone the same presentation about you, your company, the area, features, neighborhood facilities, or the quality of their investment will have vastly different results.

For those people that actually are looking for a new or different home – or possibly their very first home – the sooner you discover their motivations and learn what their real agenda is, the quicker you can begin helping them search for the new home that will meet their needs.

Still, their decision as to what to do and how to proceed could mean that any potential purchase or agreement with you to list and market their current home might be months away.

Therefore, devoting the same amount of time to working with everyone – and especially committing a lot of time to working with those who are unlikely to ever make a decision – is not a productive or effective use of your time and energy.

Be Wary Of Repeated Contacts

Sometimes it's those people who have no intention or desire of ever making a decision that keep calling you, emailing you, or asking you to show them more and more properties.

Just because someone keeps showing apparent interest by continuing to contact you doesn't necessarily mean that they will eventually buy a home from you or have you list their present home.

In fact, the opposite is probably true.

You'd like to think that when people contact or reach out to you again and again that it means that they really like you, what you offer, and the homes you are able to show them. However, this isn't always the case.

Some people will be able to make a decision on their first outing with you or on your initial presentation, but many will take more than one contact before they commit to work with you or decide on a new home.

So just returning to your office to meet with you, calling you on the phone, texting or emailing you, asking you to show them more properties, or having you do additional research on ways to market their home are not buying signs in themselves, and it may even indicate that a sale or listing is not likely or possible.

You may have noticed that some people may contact you repeatedly, attend your open houses, or ask you to show them several properties yet never seem ready to make a decision – while others who seem to show a lot of interest will end up buying a home directly from a builder or a private party without even involving you.

Why You Need A Rating System

Because people visiting or contacting you – or asking you to work with them – have their own agendas, timetables, criteria, and levels of interest, you need a way of keeping tabs on the most interested ones at any given time.

I know that there are some people who can remember and retain information about all of their customers in their heads – maybe you're one of them.

They can recall every important detail about their customers and manage all of the communication details that are necessary to produce a sale or listing.

However, even at this, it's challenging to prioritize which customers require more attention than others without mentally reviewing each individual customer – one at a time. This can be quite time consuming.

As we get older and as we continue to see and talk with more and more people, our ability to keep track of everyone and all of the little details about each customer in our heads – if we ever had that ability – becomes more of an issue.

Thus, one option is to continue to use a mental rating system where you attempt to remember who you're working with and where they are in their decision-making process – again if you ever had this ability at all.

Or, you can create a written system that eliminates the chance that someone may slip through the cracks.

Personally and professionally, I recommend the *written* system.

Go With The Written System

Your system doesn't need to be *computerized*, and it doesn't need to be expensive to create or implement, but you do need some formal way of writing down and keeping track of the contact information and other details about the people you've met.

Regardless of how many people you might be working with at any given time, the best way to make sure that you haven't forgotten any details or anything that needs to be done or scheduled is to write it down.

Then, you need to have a way of assigning a *score*, a rating, or some type of a grade to each customer.

This is how you'll indicate which ones are the closest to making a decision to buy or list, which ones are more distant, and which ones probably will never make a decision – regardless of how interested they may seem.

Without a written record of each customer, it is nearly impossible to make notes, assign and update ratings, and keep track of their progress.

The Reason For Scoring

You need to assign a grade or score to all of your leads and customers to help you prioritize and identify where each person is in their decision-making process, but there's nothing special or magical about the actual grade, score, rating, or ranking that you assign to each customer or customer unit.

It's what the rating or grade indicates.

The reason you grade, score, or rank each customer is to allow you to immediately identify – and then focus on – those customers that are the most likely at any given time to be in a position to make a decision to purchase a home from you or give you the listing.

Think of the grade as a type of shorthand or notation that will tell you at a glance just how likely someone is to purchase from you or list – and more specifically where that next sale or listing might be coming from.

It also allows other people in your company – an associate, assistant, manager, broker, or office staff – to use your notes and assist you when you're busy with other customers or away from the office.

Be diligent in deciding on which grade or score to assign to each customer.

The higher the grade, the more likely and quicker the decision will be – but only if it truly is representative of someone's interest level and ability to make a decision.

You should never force or exaggerate a grade just for the sake of appearance.

It's just that simple.

What The Score Really Means

There are many rating systems in use around the country for keeping track of how "*good*" someone is.

You probably already have some type of rating system – such as "A-B-C," "1-2-3," "hot-warm-cold," or something similar – to differentiate your customers and indicate the apparent quality of your traffic.

Regardless of which system you use, however, the best score or grade should indicate which customers are the closest to making a purchasing or listing decision.

The grade only reflects someone's willingness or ability to make a decision – and nothing else.

However, understanding their willingness and ability to purchase a home from you or list with you is huge.

The Score Is Not Personal

The rating must not be based on anything personal.

It has nothing to do with anyone personally or how well you might like or relate to someone.

It refers *solely* to the general likelihood of someone making a decision – and the approximate timing of it.

It shouldn't focus on their personality, how they dress, the car they drive, what you might have in common with them, how well you interact with them, their attitude, or how nice you think they are as a person.

Determining Who Needs Your Time

When you meet or talk with a new customer for the first time, you ask them questions and discuss their needs, requirements, and timing.

This might be in your office, at an open house, on the telephone when they call for information, or by email when someone contacts you through your website.

Now, you need a way of noting or remembering which customers are sincerely interested in doing something – and more specifically working with you.

Which people should you devote more time to and actively pursue because they are likely to purchase or list their home with you?

Conversely, which customers need minimal or virtually no contact because they have little or no interest in doing anything – or a decision seems unlikely?

How can you differentiate the levels of interest among your customers after your initial conversation with them?

The answers to these questions are found in effectively rating each customer according to their willingness and ability to buy a new home or list their current one – and more specifically to work with you to do it.

Relying On A Rating System

You need a rating system that is easy to use that allows you to determine very quickly who is deserving of your time, attention, and continuing contact after your initial meeting or conversation.

Then you can commit and plan your time to work with those customers who have the highest probability of making a decision on a new home.

While your memory may be great, you really do need a way of reviewing and managing your traffic – something you can look at and refer to frequently.

This is why you need to have a formal, written system of keeping track of your customers – even if it's just kept in a 3-ring notebook or on notecards in a drawer or box.

In addition, there are many software programs available to help you keep track of your customers.

However, they're no *substitute* for knowing how to supply the appropriate grade to each customer based upon your interaction with each customer and the answers they provide to your discovery questions.

Remember that it's the person doing the rating – you – and how the ratings are used that's important, and not whether the actual customer records are stored in a file drawer, notebook, or on a computer.

Selecting A Good System

Make sure you select a good rating system, and the one that I'll show you in the coming pages is the best for several reasons that you'll see as I explain it.

A good rating system will allow you to identify and work with those people closest to making a decision as well as those who need a little "hand-holding" along the way.

You'll also be able to identify those people that essentially require no additional contact from you.

Many people will have no interest in getting a new home, in actually listing their present home, or in working with you — and you may even wonder why they contacted or met with you at all.

Others will require minimal contact over several months, or even longer, before a decision is ever likely.

Why would you want to invest much of your time in working with these people when you know that your efforts would be more productive elsewhere?

Your rating system will let you prioritize your follow-up, and you can devote more time to those who need your help and encouragement to make a decision.

By using your rating system to identify where purchasing or listing decisions are the most likely to happen, you will be able to make those sales and secure listings that otherwise might be overlooked or go unmade because you lost track of them — thereby avoiding a loss to you, your company, and your customers.

An Essential Sales Tool

The rating system is not something that is just nice to have.

It is an essential sales and management tool.

A rating system allows you to keep track of where everyone is in the process of looking for a new home or listing their present one — from very close to making a decision to likely never to make a decision.

It lets you prioritize your time and your efforts to focus on working with just those customers closest to making a decision.

When you have written information on your customers, you can review your individual customer ratings as often as you like and update them as necessary.

This takes all of the guesswork out of identifying the people most likely to purchase or list with you — and lets you determine those that you can effectively set aside.

It truly allows you to focus on working with people who have the highest probability of making a decision with you — whether that decision is imminent or weeks or even months away.

2

The "Ready, Willing, And Able" Test

The "A-B-C" Rating System

A common format for a customer rating system in use in many new home and realty offices across the country is the "A-B-C" system.

In this format, the "A" designates the top quality or those most-likely-to-make a decision, and "C" the least prepared – with "B" somewhere in between. Sometimes, there is a "D" or even other letters also.

However, there are wide variations as to what constitutes each grade and how they are applied. For instance, what may be an "A" to one broker or agent may not be to another.

Often there are differences — and sometimes disagreements — within the same company or agency as to what each letter grade means and why someone should receive a certain grade and not another.

This variance and uncertainty underscores the need for an objective rating system rather than a subjective one.

An Objective Test Is Vital

The ratings and the rating system should not be based on anything personal and must not be reflective of someone's personality or demeanor.

A rating system must remain objective.

If anyone else in your company or your office were to review your notes on any particular customer, all should arrive at essentially the same rating for that person.

It may not be that way today, but that's the goal of an objective system.

There just is no room for subjectivity.

This will undermine a rating system quicker than anything else — except not using one at all.

The ratings must be consistently applied to all your traffic and be based solely on an objective set of measurable criteria that reflect someone's ability to make a decision and how soon that might happen.

Your emotions or personal views can't have anything to do with the ratings.

We're all human, and some of our feelings may creep into how we interpret someone's ability and willingness to make a decision, but to the extent possible, we need to be objective in our approach.

Creating The Objective Test

If the ratings that we use to evaluate the interest level and decision-making ability of our customers are truly objective, they should be true regardless of who the customers are, how many people are going to be living in the new home, and who is doing the rating.

One of the best tests to use to objectively determine the status of your customers is the "*ready, willing, and able*" test.

While the "A-B-C" system is so often used to reflect this assessment or test, there can be general confusion about what constitutes these three attributes and just how to apply them.

This is largely true because they aren't viewed as the objective measurement that they really are.

The "Ready, Willing, And Able" Test

The foundation of any good rating system is an objective set of criteria.

The best set of criteria I've found for determining someone's likelihood of making a purchasing or listing decision is the "*ready, willing, and able*" test.

It turns out that each of the three measures ("ready," "willing," and "able") indicates someone's *preparedness* or *capacity* to make a decision, and each of these can be quantified.

That is, each can be measured *objectively* as to whether it has been met — without any subjectivity being necessary.

This is the real power of this system.

So, instead of just having a good or not-so-good feeling about someone and their ability to buy or list a home with you, you actually can assess their ability on an objective basis.

And If it's truly an objective assessment, anyone who evaluates the "ready, willing, and able" criteria of a particular customer should arrive at essentially the same conclusion concerning their ability to make a decision and the timing of that decision.

The "Ready" Factor

The first test in the measurement trilogy is "READY," and this is a *physical* issue.

This means that in order for someone to be considered "ready" to make a decision on a new home, they need to be *physically* prepared to do so.

Their current residence is not and will not be a condition or determining factor in making their decision.

Their present home is not an excuse. It won't inhibit a decision.

For people looking to acquire a new home, they won't need to sell their present home prior to making a decision. In fact, their home purchase might be an investment, or they will keep their current home as a rental.

For people wanting to list their present home, deciding to make improvements to the home or fix it up first before listing it aren't necessary and won't delay their decision to put their home on the market.

This is how the "ready" test is applied and what it means.

It really is that simple.

The "Readiness" Question

To test someone's "readiness" to make a decision, you need to know if they can actually proceed – either on a new home or their current home – without the present home being a deterrent to that decision.

Notice that the key to whether this test is accomplished is the ability of someone to make the decision.

The test does not depend on the timing or ability of people to close or move into their new home. It's just whether the decision can be made.

You're only looking for someone who can give you a binder and write an offer or enter into a listing agreement with you without falling back on their present home as factoring into or governing that decision.

This is all that you need to satisfy the "ready" criteria – whether it's a purchase or listing situation.

People are still free to dispose of their present home before closing on or moving into their new home they're purchasing with you – or to make minor cosmetic improvements to their exiting home while it's on the market with you.

In fact, you might even get them an offer to purchase before those changes are undertaken or completed.

When you ask someone you're working with to purchase a home from you, you don't want to hear them tell you: *"I need to sell my current home first,"* or *"I can't do anything until I sell the home I have now,"* or *"I have to sell my present home before I can do anything."*

As long as you don't hear anything about the sale or disposition of their current home as a condition of buying their new home, they are "ready" to make a decision.

The Listing Exception

The same goes for the listing.

As long as you don't hear anything about them needing to make repairs or improvements to their current home as a condition of putting it on the market, they are "ready" to make a decision.

The exception would be if you allow a home inspection before or as a condition of the listing and work is necessary to make the home more saleable – or at a higher price – you would want to wait to advertise the home or put it in the MLS until those repairs or improvements had been made.

However, this doesn't mean that you couldn't get an approved listing agreement – the effective date would just need to be delayed or be contingent upon the repairs being undertaken and completed.

In this way, you can still get the decision, and the readiness condition would be met.

The "Willing" Component

The second part of the three-step rating formula is "WILLING." This is an *emotional* or *psychological* factor or measurement.

Someone needs to be emotionally or psychologically prepared to make the decision on buying a new home (or even their first one) or selling their current one because they *definitely* have decided to move.

It's no longer just a case of "thinking about" or wishing for a new home but actually *needing* one.

When someone makes the emotional commitment to leave the residence that they have now and move into a different home, the move actually will occur.

This is true whether it's a brand new home, just a newer home than they currently have, or even one in another location or neighborhood.

It's also true about listing the home that they have now. It's no longer a case of just putting it on the market to see if they can get their price or finding out if they can sell their present home to allow them the freedom to pursue something else. It's now a must-sell situation.

The Current Home Dilemma

When someone is "willing" to move into a new home, they will have passed the point-of-no-return, and remaining in their present home or apartment will not be a viable option.

It won't even be a consideration.

Up until the point when the "willingness" factor has been satisfied, many people will gauge what they see in the marketplace against their present home.

They'll be evaluating, comparing, and interpreting what they see in light of their present home and what it will take to replace the home they have now from a financial, lifestyle, layout, comfort, and convenience standpoint or basis.

Until the willingness factor has been satisfied, their current home often will look more attractive or appealing to them than anything else they've seen or that you might show them.

As a result, they may decide just to remain in their current home and to give up the idea of moving – and of putting their home on the market.

Whether they decide on remodeling or not, you won't get a listing or sale in such cases.

The Importance Of "Willingness"

"Willingness" is the most crucial test of someone's ability to make a decision.

Of course, being "ready" and "able" are important parts of assessing how likely, prepared, or capable someone is to make a purchasing or selling decision.

It's just that the decision won't happen – or it won't survive a cancellation or rescission – unless someone is emotionally willing to make it.

This makes "willing" the *pivotal test* in measuring how likely a sale or listing is to occur.

It's what you need to look for the most.

It's what you need for a decision to happen.

You must identify it to have a successful transaction.

In the emotional impact of the moment as you are helping your customers get excited about the possibilities of purchasing a home you are showing them or talking with them about listing their home and moving on, they may join in your excitement and decide to buy or list.

However, if they weren't already "willing" or predisposed to make that decision before they met with you and made it simply on impulse or because of their temporary excitement in how you were presenting your opportunity, they most likely will cancel or rescind their decision within a day or two.

Elimination Of "Buyer's Remorse"

The concept of "*buyer's remorse*" – where people decide to cancel or rescind their decision after you leave them and they're alone to rethink what they have done – should never be a serious issue for you if the people you are selling to or working with are emotionally prepared to make their decisions.

If they truly are "willing" to make that purchasing or listing decision when you are working with them, then it won't be a case of them having been pressured or talked into doing something that they weren't prepared to do.

While people might decide that a different type of home could meet their needs better than what they have selected with you, that they really couldn't afford their purchase ("able"), or that they really shouldn't have listed it for the price they did, they generally won't cancel a purchase or listing for remorse if they were emotionally ready ("willing") to make the decision in the first place.

Until people are emotionally, psychologically, or intently ready ("willing") to purchase a different home from what they have at the time, and nothing short of getting that home will solve their needs, the other two criteria – "ready" and "able" – are not that important.

The decision to get a new home may be based on any number of considerations – such as financial, floor plan, design, age of the home, location, lifestyle, or space and size requirements – but there must be a psychological or emotional basis for that decision.

Buying a home is largely an emotional decision.

That's why the "willingness" part of the equation is the central measure.

To have truly happy and excited homeowners, they have to be emotionally and psychologically prepared to say "*yes*" to what you're offering them. This will largely eliminate any feelings of regret about the decision.

The "ready" and "able" factors are important, but "willing" is the key to the decision.

The "Willingness" Question

No matter how much someone "thinks" that they want a new home or how many times they go back to look at it – and how ready or able they might seem to make a decision – the real issue is how much they "want" or "need" to have a new home.

When someone sees something that they like that meets their needs – regardless of whether they expected to or not – can they say "*yes*"?

This is the real issue; this is how the "willing" test is applied.

The same is true about listing their current home. Have they reached the point-of-no-return where they are ready to move, no matter what?

To be "willing" to make a decision they need to have made the mental or emotional commitment to acquire a new home or put their present home on the market *before* meeting with you.

In the case of someone looking for a seasonal residence, the "willingness" factor can be the difference as to whether a decision occurs.

If they haven't definitely decided to buy an additional home or don't know exactly what they want or where they want it, there will no purchasing decision.

Many people will contact you or engage you and you'll wonder why they even made the effort – because they seem to have no interest in getting a new home or selling their current one. They just want to look at homes or "think about" selling their present one – they might even do this more than once.

Clearly, they are not "willing" to make a decision, and no sale (purchase or listing) will ever happen — no matter how much they say they want or need to do something.

The "Able" Variable

Then there is "ABLE." This is the *financial* assessment or measurement.

The "able" test may be the *hardest* one for you to determine.

People can *act* like they can afford what they tell you they want to spend, or they can keep from disclosing important aspects of their credit report that will make them ineligible to get financing — and you may not learn about this until late in the purchasing process.

In some cases, they may not be aware of just how much home they can afford or the degree of their credit-worthiness.

"Able" means that someone can pay cash for their purchase or that they have the credit worthiness to secure a mortgage loan at a reasonable rate to move forward with their purchase and have the sale funded.

It also means that they can give you cash, a check, or credit card for the initial binder with their written offer.

Part One Of Being "Able"

This test of being "able" is met in two parts.

First, the customer must be capable of making a decision on a new home by having the financial resources to tender an initial deposit with their offer to purchase – without anything else being a factor such as selling their present home first or liquefying stocks, bonds, CDs, or other instruments.

This can be a cash deposit or a check – or even a credit card, if you accept them. It doesn't even need to be the full deposit in order to get the paperwork started.

However, to really be deemed "able," the full deposit must be tendered within the time allotted by your purchase agreement.

Otherwise, the purchase can't proceed and the "able" test will have failed.

Part Two Of Being "Able"

This "able" test also means that people have the financial ability to qualify for a loan and to repay it.

This applies to the total financial commitment of owning the home you are selling them and not just the total purchase price.

This includes closing costs, prepays, and monthly obligations like taxes, insurance, memberships, and their homeowner's association.

It could also mean that they have cash on hand or they will be using the proceeds from the sale of their current home to reinvest in a new home.

Looks Can Be Deceiving

Looks can be deceiving. You can't tell just by looking whether someone is "able."

Stating what you expect as an initial deposit or asking a general question about their credit worthiness may help you determine how "able" someone is to make a decision and purchase their new home.

However, it's possible that they will not know the answer to your question or that they will tell you what they think you want to hear.

Getting a general idea of someone's ability to qualify for a mortgage loan with your lender is an entirely appropriate question that you should be asking.

You can ask them a question about any issues that they might have in their credit report that could affect their getting a mortgage loan. You don't need to know the details – just if they exist.

If such issues exist, you can give your lender a "heads-up" or choose to work with a lender who might be more appropriate for working successfully with such issues.

Remaining Objective

The powerful part about the "ready, willing, and able" test is that it is OBJECTIVE – if you allow it to be.

Without trying to add *shades* or degrees of whether someone is "ready" or "willing" or "able," the test is a straightforward, objective one.

Nevertheless, the interpretation of it and its actual application often means that many people are misjudged on their ability to make a decision to buy or sell.

As a result, some people are afforded too much attention and considered more qualified to make a decision than they really are – because of how they appear or the way they talk.

Sometimes, just the interest people appear to show can make them seem more qualified than they really are.

Conversely, others who actually are capable of making a decision may be ignored or pursued less diligently.

Your personal feelings about how "good" someone is cannot be allowed to enter into your rating.

How well you like or dislike someone – or whatever interests you may have in common with them – should have no bearing on the grade you give them.

The key to the successful use of the "ready, willing, and able" test is to remain objective.

Getting Consistent Results

If the "ready, willing, and able" test is not applied objectively or evenly, you won't get a consistent rating for your customers, and your sales process – including your follow-up – will be less effective.

You need to know and be able to trust that whatever grade or score you apply to someone will immediately tell you – and any others on your team that might occasionally help you – what the likelihood is of them making a decision at any moment.

This is how you will strategize your time and efforts to work the most effectively and efficiently with the traffic that you have – so that you can produce the sales and listings that are possible.

Remember that someone either satisfies each of the three criteria completely or they don't.

There's no "partial" or "almost" to it. This is how the grading is applied.

It’s easy to let someone’s speech, appearance, or actions influence how you treat them.

If someone is dressed neatly or groomed well, or polite or pleasant, there may be a tendency to treat them more credibly or to not question their abilities as much as you might with someone who looks or acts less likely to be ready to make a decision.

Putting It All Together

It doesn’t matter how well you like someone or how well you interact with them while you are sitting with them in your office, looking at properties, or in their home.

You just need to ask yourself the ready, willing, and able questions for each person and answer them honestly.

No fudging — just an honest assessment. It really is that simple.

If someone can make a decision without their present home being a factor (notice I didn’t say close or move into their new home but only make the decision), they are “ready.”

If they are emotionally capable or prepared to make such a decision because their current living situation just doesn’t meet their needs or offer them the comfort or lifestyle they desire, then they are “willing.”

Finally, if they have the financial or credit resources to move forward, they are "able."

Put all three measurements together, and the customer you're working with has satisfied the "ready, willing, and able" test.

There is nothing mysterious or difficult about the "ready, willing, and able" test.

It is a set of objective criteria that will help you assess someone's ability to make a decision on a new home.

Keep personalities out of the equation and focus just on the facts.

Then you can allocate your time accordingly to work with those people who are the most likely to make a purchasing decision.

3

An "A" Rating Isn't Sufficient

Committing To A Rating System

If you've read this far, and you're not already using some type of a formal rating system, you really should begin doing so.

There's no time like right now to get started.

This is particularly true if you are serious about making more sales and working with the customers most inclined to make a decision.

You need to be able to keep track of your customers and identify which ones require your attention or your focus – and which ones need little or no attention.

The timesavings alone makes it worthwhile.

Then you can allocate your energy where it will do the most good – working with those who are the closest to making a decision as well as those who could be ready to make a decision soon – with a little coaching and encouragement from you.

Some salespeople just keep track of their best customers in their head and don't worry too much about the rest of their customers.

Others make random notes about their customers but don't employ a formal way of rating customers or keeping track of the notes they've made.

Regardless of what you've been using so far for a rating system, keep an open mind as you read this chapter.

I've promised you a revolutionary, rating system, and by the end of this chapter, you'll see just how special it is.

It's a simple, yet powerful, system that will allow you to produce more listings and sales (making you more money) and manage your time more effectively (saving wasted or unproductive activity).

Identifying Your Top Possibilities

Depending on how many people you see or talk with in a week, it may seem easy to keep track of the one or two top customers without formally rating them.

But, are you sure just *how* good they are and that they are the only ones you should be focusing on?

It's easy to misjudge people and their interest level in an initial meeting. That's why an objective set of criteria is important, and that's why a formal rating system that uses such criteria is useful.

You can give someone an "A" rating or mark them "hot" based on what seemed to be their level of interest and your "feeling" about them.

However, you really need to apply the "ready, willing, and able" test to verify that they are as good as you think they are and that you're not just *wishing* them into an "A" or top rating.

Using The "A-B-C" Rating System

Again, the basis of any quality rating system needs to be a set of objective criteria, and the "ready, willing, and able" test seems to meet our requirements.

Since you already may be using an "A-B-C" rating system (or a variation of it), let's discuss how to apply those grades or scores using the "ready, willing, and able" formula.

Keep in mind that even when something like this "ready, willing, and able" rating test is used, there often are wide variations in the results – due largely to the fact that the test may be only loosely applied and then used subjectively rather than objectively.

Using this "A-B-C" rating system, a customer who is ready, willing, and able to make a decision on listing their current home or purchasing a new home – with no conditions or contingencies – would be rated as an "**A**."

There should be absolutely no guesswork, "feeling," or interpretation about whether someone "deserves" an "A" rating.

Either someone satisfies all three of the tests or they don't. If they do, they're an "A." It's that simple.

However, if you are working with someone who is otherwise prepared to make a decision on their home, and you use a financing or any other type of contingency to help them start the paperwork, it's the same as not having any conditions – and the customer still would be rated as an "A."

If *one* of the criteria has not been met or satisfied – such as not being sure what they actually want in a new home, needing to sell their present home, or wanting to "think about" what they've seen – a "**B**" would apply.

If *two or more* of the "ready, willing, and able" criteria are missing, those customers would be rated a "**C**."

Adding A "D" To The Rating System

People who are not seriously looking for a new home – as well as those who are not or will not be in a position to make a decision on selling their present home or buying another home – would be rated as a "**D.**"

This could include those who do not have sufficient income to qualify to purchase a home that reasonably meets their stated needs, ones who can't get approved for financing, those who recently acquired another home and have no interest in another in the foreseeable future, people moving out of your area, those visiting your area, those who insist on listing their home for an unrealistic amount, or those upside down on their home.

However, using just the basic "A," "B," "C," and "D" grades is not SUFFICIENT.

You won't get the total picture using just this system, and just adding more letter grades won't help either.

Adjusting Your Rating System

The "ready, willing, and able" test is fine as far as it goes, but there is one key component missing for a totally effective and efficient rating system.

You must know how well someone LIKES working with you and what they think you can bring to the relationship.

This one addition makes all the difference in getting a sale or listing — and in apportioning your time.

It allows you to focus your efforts on identifying and working just with those people who like what you can offer them. They will be more likely to do business with you than those people who are indifferent or don't particularly care for you or your company.

If people don't like what you are offering them or don't feel that you can meet their needs, they are not likely to decide to work with you — no matter what you do or how hard you try.

Effort Is Not The Answer

Regardless of how many times you call, write, email, or text someone who has looked at homes with you, if they don't like what you can do for them or don't care for your company, they are not going to work with you.

Simply put, what you bring to the table just doesn't work for them or satisfy their needs.

In cases like these, your effort has nothing to do with making a sale or producing a listing. In fact, how nice or professional you are, how often you communicate with your customers, what you are prepared to do for and with them, the quality of your listings, or how hard you try will have little effect.

So while someone might truly be "ready, willing, and able," this just indicates that they are capable of making a decision to list their home or get another and likely will be able to do so quickly – certainly within 30 days (and possibly even within a day or two).

However, without the "LIKEABILITY" factor being present, when such a decision is made to move forward, it will not involve you, your company, or your listings.

Introducing The "A-1" Rating

Finding someone prepared to make a decision who satisfies the "ready, willing, and able" criteria is a great start.

However, you need to make sure that they want to work with you, that you can meet their needs with what you can show them, and that they like you before you can make the sale or get the listing.

And the way that you determine this is by *asking* and *listening*.

Then, you need to have a way of keeping track of those customers who are "ready, willing, and able" to make a decision quickly on listing their current home or getting a new home who also LIKE the idea of working with you.

This one distinction makes all the difference in your ratings – and ultimately in your sales efficiency.

Take an "A" customer that meets the "ready, willing, and able" criteria and then add the suffix "**1**" to their grade if they like your abilities and would like to work with you.

Now they become an ***"A-1"*** customer – the best chance you have for getting a purchasing or listing decision at any given moment.

This one change will make an enormous difference in how you work with your traffic, and you will be more effective and efficient.

Refining The Traditional Ratings

You won't be eliminating the traditional "A," "B," "C," and "D" ratings.

You are just creating the additional, modified ratings of *"A-1," "B-1," "C-1,"* and *"D-1"* to refine and improve your rating system.

Thus, as you review your traffic and formulate your contact strategy for each customer, you now can choose to allocate your time and resources to maintain contact with just those customers who have the highest probability of actually working with you to purchase their new home or list their existing one – those you have given the additional designation of *"1"* after their letter grade.

This especially applies to those top customers who are capable of purchasing or listing within the next 30 days (or less) – your newly defined "A-1" customers.

In addition to having a customer who is "ready, willing, and able" to make a decision quickly, you now can differentiate between an "A" (who isn't inclined to work with you) and an "A-1" customer who *likes* you well enough to want to work with you.

Furthermore, your "B," "C," and "D" customers who like you well enough to want to work with you to buy their next home or sell their existing one will become *"B-1,"* *"C-1,"* and *"D-1"* customers, respectively.

Applying The "A-1" Rating Objectively

Just as it is with the "ready, willing, and able" test, you want to make sure that the test for the "1" rating is objective and not a subjective one.

You can't invent "A-1" customers at will.

You can't wish someone into an "A-1" rating just because you want to make a sale or get a listing.

You can't call someone who really is an "A" an "A-1" just because you like them or think they are a strong "A" – or because you think you need to have an "A-1" customer to work with.

You can't just use it to indicate that you think someone will make a decision quickly.

Remain objective throughout the rating process.

The "A-1" rating must only be used when all four attributes are present – ready, willing, able, *and* like – and not as a way of flagging or elevating an otherwise non-"A-1" customer.

Giving You An Edge With Your Time

This enhanced rating system that I am giving you provides an edge in planning how to organize your day and how you schedule your follow-up contact with your customers.

You no longer need to pursue or concentrate on those people who aren't likely to work with you no matter how hard you try. They simply don't like your approach or don't think that you can meet their needs – and no amount of additional contact is going to change that.

Instead, you can devote your time and energies to working just with those customers who are the most likely to list their home or buy with you.

So, each day when you are deciding who you need to work with – in the limited amount of time you have available – you should start with your "A-1" customers.

They require the most immediate attention, and because now you have clearly marked who they are, you can concentrate on working with them.

After that, you can work with your top "B-1" and "C-1" customers to see what you can do to help them satisfy the issues keeping them from a decision and move them along toward an "A-1" rating.

Under this plan, you won't be focusing on your "A," "B," and "C" customers, and you will have limited contact with them.

This is the revolutionary rating system that will allow you to produce more sales and save time.

Hoarding Isn't The Answer

Just having several top-ranked customers on file in your desk drawer or database because you feel good about them is not the way to make more sales.

Some rely on this so much that they actually have long lists or a big stack of cards of such customers.

They hoard what they believe to be their top customers – without doing anything to facilitate a decision.

They act as if these people always are going to be interested and ready to do something with them.

Regardless of whether these people have been correctly rated as someone who actually will buy or sell, or just identified because of a "feeling," keeping a bunch of names on file with no action to support their high rating will only cause disappointment – and produce no sales.

People Are Subject To Change

Keeping large stacks of cards or computer records on file of "good" customers who will "surely buy or sell someday" without reaching out to those people or maintaining regular contact with them is just wasting potential sales opportunities.

Such a policy assumes that people don't change over time, but obviously, they can and do.

An "A" or "A-1" customer from 6 months ago likely has already done something by now (especially if the rating was done correctly) – and keeping them on file as a potential sale or listing is just wishful thinking.

An "A-1" *Is* Special

Using my new rating system, an "A-1" customer is the best one that you can work with at any particular time because they *like* you and are *ready* to make a quick decision – and very likely with you.

However, it doesn't mean that this is automatic.

It still takes work because you'll be in competition with other brokers and even homebuilders that also appeal to your customers and can address their needs.

If you truly are grading your customers properly, you should have no more than one or two "A-1" customers at any given time. This makes them very special.

On occasion, you might not have any "A-1"s, and that's OK – it's temporary.

If you have more than a couple of "A-1"s at any one time, you likely are not being diligent enough in your ratings or in pursuing the sale or listing.

An "A-1" customer is extremely important to you. However, you can't produce them at will or wish them into existence, and there is nothing automatic about making a sale to an "A-1."

The True "A-1" Customer

The true "A-1" customer is in position to make a buying or selling decision right now – on this appointment.

Therefore, you are in a race against the clock with all the other brokers, homebuilders, or homes for-sale-by-owner that also can meet their needs.

Time truly is of the essence.

There may not be another chance to make a sale or get a listing with the "A-1" customer "tomorrow."

Make it today, if possible – on this appointment or showing.

Enjoying Success With The "A-1"

You should have a very high closing rate with your "A-1" customers because of your commitment to them and the relationships that you are building with them.

Nothing is automatic, but if the sale or listing seems imminent while you're talking with them or showing them properties, don't put it off until a later meeting or conversation.

You may not get another chance to close the sale or listing with those customers.

Don't risk losing a listing or sale to anyone else.

Your "A-1" customers are your best chance for sales success at any moment.

Special Contact For Your "A"s

In addition to your normal written and telephone post-visit contact, one more step is necessary for just your "A" customers – not your "A-1"s or any other ratings.

The presumption is that that these "A" rated customers already bought something else or listed with someone else – or you wouldn't have rated them an "A."

Wait until 30 days have elapsed since your initial meeting or conversation with them, and then telephone just your "A" customers again to learn what they bought or who they listed with – and to discuss it with them.

However, if they didn't choose another broker and still want to sell their current home or get another, evaluate why they have not made a decision and re-grade them accordingly. You still might be able to work with them.

Adding Your Congratulations

When you talk with your "A" customers, you'll have an opportunity to congratulate them on their purchasing decision and ask why they selected what they did and how they think it will meet their needs.

This is an important gesture and will differentiate you from your competition.

Be sincere in your congratulations and earnest in learning why they chose what they did. Try to find out how it differs from what you might have shown them.

Also, be sure to send them a congratulations card or email. This should be professional and sincere as well.

There should be no expression of disappointment since you knew when you met them that you didn't hit it off with them.

Simply tell them that you enjoyed getting to know them and offer your assistance for them or any of their friends should they need it.

An "A" customer may seem like a "lost sale" because they worked with someone else, but you weren't seriously in the running for their business.

By expressing a sincere happiness for their decision, you will create good will and a potential ambassador that can produce future referrals.

Focusing On Your "A"s Again

If you learn from talking with your "A" customers, when you call them a month after your initial conversation or meeting, that they haven't made a decision because their timing or expectations changed – or that they really weren't "ready, willing, and able" after all – re-grade them to what seems appropriate.

They might be interested in working with you now (which would add a "1" to their new, revised grade).

It's quite possible that their expectations changed and now your approach seems more reasonable to them.

If they decided to rent, learn when their lease expires and plan on talking with them a couple of times prior to then to find out how you can help them in their search for a new home.

Rating With All Four Factors

To be an "A-1" customer, all four tests must be satisfied: ready, willing, able, *and* like.

This is the only rating where the answers to all four questions will be – and must be – "Yes."

The other ratings ("A," "B," "B-1," "C," "C-1," "D," and "D-1") are directly dependent on the objective answers to these four questions or tests as well – and reflect that at least one of the answers is "*No.*"

Also, be careful not to misrank someone because you are not establishing a good rapport with them, or they don't like your listings or your approach to marketing their home – especially if they are someone who appears to be serious about making a decision.

An "A" customer who is ready, willing, and able to make a decision on their new home but does not like your approach or who needs something significantly different than what you can show them may well go someplace else within a few days (or even later that same day) and make a decision with someone else.

Many salespeople have a tendency to call such a customer a "D" because they are unable to address their needs.

This is not correct and will lead to an inaccurate analysis of your traffic history and quality – and yield missed opportunities for your post-visit follow-up contact.

Begin adding the "1" rating to the appropriate letter grade to denote those customers who like you, your company, and your approach to sales and marketing – and focus your time and efforts on helping them to reach their decisions.

This is the real power of this rating system.

You will become more effective, efficient, and productive as a result.

4

Going Behind The Score

Knowing The Scoring Possibilities

As we just discussed in the previous chapter, there are eight possible ratings or scores that you will use to initially categorize someone's level of interest in purchasing a new home or in listing their current one.

This rating is subject to change as you learn more about your customers and how you might be able to help them or work them, but this is where the assessment begins.

The scoring or rating is based on applying the "ready," "willing," and "able" test to your customers and then using the new test with the suffix "1" that I have given you for indicating "like" when it applies.

Four of the grades show a general interest.

Four indicate a preference for working with you and your company.

The four *general interest* ratings are "**A**," "**B**," "**C**," and "**D**." These scores, grades, rankings, or ratings denote various levels of interest and ability to act but do not signify that they want to do business with you.

The four *specific interest* ratings that you'll use to indicate that people are inclined to work with you to buy another property or sell their existing home are "**A-1**," "**B-1**," "**C-1**," and "**D-1**." These scores, grades, rankings, or ratings also denote various levels of interest and ability to act, but they signify that people are willing to do business with you.

Applying The "A" Score

Through a series of various discovery questions, you can help yourself determine your customer's score or rating.

You are attempting to measure three variables – "ready," "willing," and "able." When you are satisfied that *all three* of these have been met, you have an "A" customer.

This means no conditions, no contingencies, and no hedging. They know what they want and are ready to make a decision immediately to purchase or to list, but it could take up to a month or so for them to do so.

An **"A"** customer (1) does not have to sell their present home before making a decision on another or doesn't need to make improvements to their current home before listing it, **and**

(2) is emotionally or psychologically ready to make a decision and move from their current home because it just doesn't meet their needs and they are tired of coping with it – or they are ready to list their current home and buy another one, **and**

(3) has the cash or funds available to tender an earnest money deposit or binder and can qualify for a mortgage loan to close on the property and take title to it – if they are listing their current home it means that they are able to pay off their current mortgage from the proceeds of the sale or from their own financial resources in the case of a shortfall.

Applying The "A-1" Score

Here again, you are attempting to measure three variables – "ready," "willing," and "able." However, you also are looking for and evaluating the presence of that all-important fourth variable.

You will be determining if "like" has been met.

When you are satisfied that all four of these questions have been answered, you have an "A-1" customer.

This means no conditions, no contingencies, and no hedging – about making a decision or about working with you. That decision could be imminent.

An **"A-1"** customer (1) does not have to sell their present home before making a decision on another or doesn't need to make improvements to their current home before listing it, **and**

(2) is emotionally or psychologically ready to make a decision and move from their current home because it just doesn't meet their needs and they are tired of coping with it – in the case of a listing, they are committed to putting their current home on the market and buying another one, **and**

(3) has the cash or funds available to tender an earnest money deposit or binder and can qualify for a mortgage loan to close on the property and take title to it – if they are listing their current home it means that they are able to pay off their current mortgage from the proceeds of the sale or from their own financial resources in the case of a shortfall, **and**

(4) likes you and your company well enough or feels that you can help them sell their current home or purchase another so that they desire to have you work with them.

It doesn't mean that the "A-1" customer is an automatic sale or listing, but this is where you are going to find your sales or listings – you have as good a chance and possibly even a better one than other agents or offices to compete for these customers.

This is your optimum customer because they have the capacity and interest to make a decision.

Applying The "B" Score

The "B" score results when one, *and only one*, of the "ready," "willing," and "able" components is missing. It can be any of the three, but typically, it is the "willing" test that is missing – as in putting off or waiting to make a decision that seems like it should be easy to make, given the facts.

A **"B"** customer (1) may need to sell their present home before making a decision on purchasing another – or desires to make improvements to their current home before listing it, **or**

(2) may not be emotionally or psychologically ready to make a decision and move from their current home or list it because they want time to think about what they are contemplating – or they are not sure what they want to do or aren't totally committed to making the decision, **or**

(3) may not have the funds available to tender an earnest money deposit or binder and may not have a

credit score sufficient to qualify for a mortgage loan to close on the property and take title to it – if they are listing their current home it means that they might not be interested in listing their home at the price you suggest or that they need to sell it for more money than the market will support.

Remember it's just *one* of those variables to which the answer is "no." The answer to the other two is "yes."

It doesn't matter which one of the three is missing, and it won't necessarily be the same factor that is missing for each "B" customer.

This often means that a month or more – sometimes even up to six months or longer – might be required to accomplish the missing variable.

Applying The "B-1" Score

Here, you are looking for the "like" factor. It will exist as a variable even though *one* of the other vital tests will be missing. This results in a score or rating of a "B-1."

Typically, it is the "willing" test that is going to be missing – showing up as a reluctance to make a decision that seems like it should be easy to make.

A **"B-1"** customer (1) may need to sell their present home before making a decision on purchasing another –

or desires to make improvements to their current home before listing it, **or**

(2) may not be emotionally or psychologically ready to make a decision and move from their current home or list it because they aren't sure what they want or aren't totally committed to making the decision, **or**

(3) may not have the funds available to tender an earnest money deposit or binder and may not have a credit score sufficient to qualify for a mortgage loan to close on the property and take title to it – if they are listing their current home it means that they might not be interested in listing their home at the price you suggest or that they need to sell it for more money than the market will support, **and**

(4) likes you and your company well enough to want to work with you as you help them work through the situation that is preventing their decision and allow them to become an "A-1."

Remember that it's just *one* of these variables to which the answer is "no." The answer to the others – including "like" – is "yes." It's just determining which one is missing and then working to alleviate that deficiency.

This often means that a month or more – sometimes even up to six months or longer – might be required to accomplish the missing variable.

Applying The "C" Score

When two or even all three of the variables have not been satisfied – but your customer still has some interest or capacity to list their home or purchase another one – you have a score or rating of a "C."

The "C" means that any combination of factors – or all of them – have yet to be satisfied. It could be "ready" and "willing," "ready" and "able," or "willing" and "able" – or all three – that are missing.

A **"C"** customer (1) likely will need to sell their present home before making a decision on purchasing another – or desires to make improvements to their current home before listing it, **and/or**

(2) likely will not be emotionally or psychologically ready to make a decision and move from their current home or list their present one because they want time to think about what they are contemplating – or they are not totally committed to making the decision or sure of what they want to do, what type of a new home they want, or when they want to make the move, **and/or**

(3) possibly may not have the funds available to tender an earnest money deposit or binder and may not have a credit score sufficient to qualify for a mortgage loan to close on the property and take title to it – if they are listing their current home it means that they might not

be interested in listing their home at the price you suggest or that they need to sell it for more money than the market will support.

Here, it's at least *two* of those variables to which the answer is "no" – and it could even be all three.

It doesn't matter which variables are missing, but such a person is far away from a decision until those issues are resolved. This often means that several months to a year or more might be required before such a customer has accomplished all of the required tests.

Applying The "C-1" Score

The big difference here is the presence of "like." Your customer still has two or even all three of the "ready-willing-and-ready" variables to satisfy, but the "like" variable is in place. This means that you have a score or rating of a "C-1."

Like the "C" rating or score, the "C-1" means that "ready" and "willing," "ready" and "able," or "willing" and "able" – or possibly all three of them – are missing. However, now the "like" variable is present.

A **"C-1"** customer (1) may need to sell their present home before making a decision on purchasing another – or desires to make improvements to their current home before listing it, **and/or**

(2) may not be emotionally or psychologically ready to make a decision and move from their current home or list their present one because they want time to think about what they are contemplating – or they are not totally committed to making the decision or sure of what they want to do, what type of a new home they want, or when they want to make the move, **and/or**

(3) may not have the funds available to tender an earnest money deposit or binder and may not have a credit score sufficient to qualify for a mortgage loan to close on the property and take title to it – if they are listing their current home it means that they might not be interested in listing their home at the price you suggest or that they need to sell it for more money than the market will support, **and**

(4) likes you personally or likes what you and your company can offer – or feels that you can help them well enough to want to work with you to help them list their present home or find another one when they have worked through the two or three missing conditions that need to be satisfied first.

At least *two* of those variables – and possibly all three of the "ready, willing, and able" ones – will be answered "no," but the "like" will be answered "yes."

It doesn't matter which variables are missing, but such a person is far away from a decision until those issues are resolved. This often means that several months to a year or more might be required before such a customer has accomplished all of the required tests.

Applying The "D" Score

A "D" score means that no decision is possible for at least a year – and maybe not even then. There are many factors that result in a "D" score, but all stem from the fact that *all three variables* cannot be met or satisfied.

A **"D"** customer (1) must sell their present home before making a decision on purchasing another but cannot or will not because they just purchased their current home, they have little to no equity in the home, they recently renovated it, it's over-improved it for the neighborhood, or the value has dropped substantially, **and**

(2) is not emotionally or psychologically ready to make a decision and move from their current home or list their present one because they just remodeled their current home, have no interest in actually moving, feel that they cannot replace what they have for what they are willing or able to invest in another home, or may consider moving out of your area, **and**

(3) does not have the financial ability or credit score to qualify for a reasonable mortgage loan amount – they might have other conditions as well such as large medical bills from a current or recent accident, illness,

or surgery; student loans; late payments; repossessions; foreclosures; bankruptcies; a short sale; loss of a job; a failed business; or not established in the area.

For the "D" all variables are missing, regardless of why. Some people are only interested in "looking" while others just don't have the resources to do anything.

Applying The "D-1" Score

A "D-1" score still means that no decision is possible for at least a year. It also means that they like you well enough to consider doing business with you – when and if that ever becomes possible.

A **"D-1"** customer (1) must sell their present home before making a decision on purchasing another but cannot or will not because they just purchased their current home, they have little to no equity in the home, or the value has dropped substantially, **and**

(2) is not emotionally or psychologically ready to make a decision and move from their current home or list it because they just remodeled their current home or feel that they cannot replace what they have for what they are willing or able to invest in another home, **and**

(3) does not have the financial ability or credit score to qualify for a reasonable mortgage loan amount – they might have other conditions as well such as large

medical bills from a current or recent accident, illness, or surgery; student loans; late payments; repossessions; foreclosures; bankruptcies; a short sale; unemployment; a failed business; or new to the area without established roots, **and**

(4) likes you personally or likes what you and your company can offer — or feels that you can help them well enough to want to work with you to help them list their present home or find another one when they have worked through all of the conditions that need to be satisfied first.

At-A-Glance Scoring Summary

"A" Ready to make a decision, **AND**
Willing to make a decision, **AND**
Able to make a decision, **AND**
Usually done very quickly — less than 30 days.

"A-1" Ready to make a decision, **AND**
Willing to make a decision, **AND**
Able to make a decision, **AND**
Likes working with you, **AND**
Usually done very quickly — less than 30 days.

"B" Ready **and** Willing, **but not** Able, **OR**
Willing **and** Able, **but not** Ready, **OR**
Able **and** Ready, **but not** Willing, **AND**
Often take 30-90 days — and as much as 180.

"B-1" Ready **and** Willing, **but not** Able, **OR**
Willing **and** Able, **but not** Ready, **OR**
Able **and** Ready, **but not** Willing, **AND**
Likes working with you, **AND**
Often take 30-90 days – and as much as 180.

"C" Ready, **but not** Willing, **and not** Able, **OR**
Willing, **but not** Able, **and not** Ready, **OR**
Able, **but not** Ready, **and not** Willing, **OR**
Not Ready, **not** Willing, **and not** Able, **AND**
Typically takes 90-365 days, or more.

"C-1" Ready, **but not** Willing, **and not** Able, **OR**
Willing, **but not** Able, **and not** Ready, **OR**
Able, **but not** Ready, **and not** Willing, **OR**
Not Ready, **not** Willing, **and not** Able, **AND**
Likes working with you, **AND**
Typically takes 90-365 days, or more.

"D" **Not** Ready, **not** Willing, **and not** Able, **AND**
Requires over a year, if ever, for a decision.

"D-1" **Not** Ready, **not** Willing, **and not** Able, **AND**
Likes working with you, **AND**
Requires over a year, if ever, for a decision.

5

Only A Few Can Be An "A-1"

The Importance Of Your "A-1"s

The most important people for you to be concentrating on each day are your "A-1" customers, but of course not everyone can be an "A-1."

In fact, very few are or ever will be.

As I stressed in Chapter 3, you might have only one or two "A-1" customers at any given time. You might have none.

That's why your "A-1" customers are so special and that's why you need to focus on getting a decision from as many of them as possible.

Strive for at least a 50% conversion ratio of your "A-1"s – that's getting a sale or listing from at least half.

However, it's not important how many "A-1" customers you have at any one time (as long as you have some throughout the year).

It's only important that you know what to do with them to maximize the possibility of making a sale.

You can't — and must not — manufacture "A-1"s by giving this designation to someone who doesn't deserve it, based on the set of four objective criteria.

Either someone is an "A-1" or they are not.

Remember that an "A-1" designation does not mean that someone *will* buy or list their home with you — just that they can and that they might. Much is still up to you.

You are in competition for their business with other brokers, homebuilders, and homes for-sale-by-owner that also can satisfy their needs — and you can't leave anything to chance.

Make Additional Contact Intentional

As important as your "A-1" customers are for your sales success, you can't count on them just contacting you when they are ready to make a decision.

You can't wait until they figure out on their own that you are the one they should be using to list or buy.

If you wait for an "A-1" just to contact you on their own, you're going to lose out.

You have to intentionally schedule all contacts after the initial meeting, know why you are scheduling it, and know what you want to accomplish.

You have to take responsibility for your customer base and schedule the appropriate next contact with each of your customers.

Non-Face-To-Face Contact

While most agents feel that they need to schedule another appointment with each customer, this idea largely is misunderstood.

It's true that you should use one appointment or contact to set the next one, but it doesn't necessarily – and usually doesn't – mean driving around with them some more or an in-person visit in your office or their home.

There are so many other types of contacts that typically are more appropriate for the majority of your customers than the physical, face-to-face meeting – because so few of them will be an "A-1."

I'm talking about emails, letters, texting, notes, postcards, and phone calls for the majority of your customers.

Over time, your frequency of contact will adjust according to the rating of your customers – and how soon they are willing to act.

However, for those people that you do need to see again relatively soon (such as your "A-1"s or those you need to work with some more before determining where they are in the process), you must intentionally schedule a return appointment or contact and not just leave it up to them.

For some of your customers you will have virtually no additional contact with them – or only an occasional telephone, email, or written contact.

For others, such as your "A-1" customers, your contact will be immediate and almost daily.

That's why this rating system is so powerful.

It lets you identify and concentrate on just those people who are close to making a decision – and not just any decision but one that involves you and your company.

Working Efficiently

If you were to devote the same amount of time, effort, and energy to all of your customers or all of the people you talk with about buying or selling – regardless of their interest level or ability to make a decision – you would have very little to show for your work.

Many people will never use you to list their current home or buy another one no matter what you do or say, and many others will never buy or sell with you although they seem to like working with you.

Spending an inordinate amount of time working with people that are not in a position to list their current home or buy another – or have no interest in doing so – will produce no tangible results.

You must not confuse activity for progress.

Your contact with your customers needs to be at a frequency and of a type – and with a message – that is appropriate for their level of interest, timing, and ability to make a decision.

So while you devote everything you can within a very short period of time – literally hours or days – to help your “A-1” customers decide that you are the most appropriate choice for them, what about the vast majority of your traffic that is not rated as “A-1”?

Most of your traffic will be rated as something other than an “A-1” and most will never reach the “A-1” level.

However, if you did nothing with your traffic except wait for the one or two “A-1”s to come along every couple of weeks, you would be missing out on so much and doing a disservice to you, your company, and your customers.

So for starters, you must be reasonably certain of the ability of each customer to make a decision and how likely that is to include you.

This will allow you to identify the occasional "A-1" and to work effectively and efficiently with the rest of your traffic.

However, this may not be so apparent on the initial appointment or outing.

Initial Post-Visit Contact

Start by sending everyone – and not just the "good" ones – a thank-you note within the initial 24 hours following their meeting with you.

Every message can be identical, and the notes or cards (or emails) can be prepared in advance.

Essentially, you just need to say three things in your note, and that is all. Thank them for contacting you, say how nice it was to meet them, and tell them that you look forward to working with them as they search for their new home. That's why all the notes can be the same – with an additional couple of words to those cards going to potential listing customers.

Save the personalization for later after you have begun to develop more of a relationship.

Then, telephone everyone within a few days of their visit – beginning with the highest rated ones first and then progressing through all of your traffic.

For best results, establish a specific day or time to call them before you finish meeting with them.

The call could even be the same day as the visit if that's what you've scheduled.

Checking On Your Initial Rating

Your post-visit phone call serves many purposes.

The first thing you do is thank them for contacting you or letting you meet with them.

Then, you can answer questions, verify and supplement information you received during the initial meeting or conversation, and establish the next contact.

Primarily though you are testing your rating.

This is why you telephone *everyone* who has visited you – to make reasonably sure that you have scored them correctly and that you can proceed accordingly.

It's also why you do it soon after the initial contact because this lets you determine the course of your post-visit contact from that point.

An Exception To The Rule

The only exception to this calling plan is when you are reasonably certain that your rating of a "D" (and not "D-1") is correct and you find little positive value to be gained through additional contact.

For instance, when someone visits your open house or otherwise contacts you and makes it very clear that they don't live in your area and wouldn't consider relocating – or that they are planning on moving out of your area to another locale – there is little to be achieved by telephoning them.

The same would be true for someone who calls on one of your listings and clearly is not really looking for a new home but just curious – maybe it's a neighbor, their former home, a former neighborhood, or just a house they drove by.

From what you learn during your initial conversation, you know that they are a "D" (again, not a "D-1") and your post-visit call – even if you could successfully contact them – would only verify what they told you and would not be a good use of your time.

They probably don't want to hear from you since they had no interest in buying a home when they contacted you or visited your open house, and you have nothing to accomplish by talking with them – unless it's just to thank them for visiting and meeting with you or to explore the possibility of them giving you a referral.

Nevertheless, don’t use the “D” rating unless it really applies, and don’t use this line of thinking to avoid calling people as you should.

Amending The Rating

If it appears – even after your phone call with your customers – that you will not be able to deliver what they are looking for or comply with their listing strategy, give them the appropriate letter grade without the “1” following it and move on to more interested people.

However, your telephone conversation with someone that appeared to be an “A,” “B,” or “C” during your initial contact – while you were talking with them at your open house or in your office, or when they called you – may change your opinion about them.

They may reveal additional information that suggests that they actually do want to work with you and that their expectations are realistic. Then, you can amend their grade to an “A-1,” “B-1,” or “C-1” – and maintain contact accordingly.

In some cases, you may not get a chance to meet with them very long or determine their actual rating during your initial meeting or conversation, and you will have to rely on this post-visit telephone call to make your assessment. This is precisely why the post-visit phone call is used.

A "C-1" is a good *default rating* when you have nothing more to go on during an initial meeting or phone call.

Scheduling Your Time

You need to make sure that you are working with those people who like you and the way you can help them well enough to eventually decide to list their current home or purchase their next home with you.

While we say that an "A" or "A-1" customer will make a decision within 30 days (and usually considerably less than that) to indicate how serious they are about making a decision, there are no similar timing parameters or suggestions that apply to the "B" or "B-1" and "C" or "C-1" customers.

It can take months or even years before some people are ready to make a decision, and some people will never be ready.

Maintaining Your Focus

During your post-visit follow-up contact with your "B-1" and "C-1" customers, your focus is identifying what issues they have that are preventing a decision.

Then you want to determine what it will take to remove those barriers to a decision – and how you can help this become a reality.

Normally, there is a ranking progression for customers who have conditions or issues that need to be met or satisfied before they can make a decision.

For instance, a "C-1" customer will progress to a "B-1" customer and then ultimately to an "A-1" customer as they become more serious about acquiring their new home – or they eliminate some of the issues and conditions that have prevented or forestalled a decision previously.

However, a "C-1" customer can skip the "B-1" step altogether and go straight to being an "A-1" if the barriers or conditions that had existed as a "C-1" have disappeared.

Even some of your "D-1" customers can work through the conditions that prevented them from being able to make a decision, and you can help make that happen.

So does every "C-1" customer move up to being a "B-1" customer? Does every "B-1" customer move to an "A-1"? Of course not. There is nothing that certain in sales.

Even if someone moves up to an "A-1" or starts out there, not every "A-1" will work with you either, but that doesn't stop you from trying to capitalize on each customer to get the greatest return possible – with the goal of getting at least half of your "A-1"s to choose to work with you.

You'll Only Close An "A-1"

As you maintain contact with each customer, you are searching for what it will take to get them to an "A-1" rating so that you can list their home or get them to make a decision on another home.

Not everyone will transition from a lower score to an "A-1."

Some people will always be a "C-1" or "D-1," and no sale will ever occur.

However, you will only get a decision to move forward with an "A-1" customer – even if they literally turn into one while you're talking with them (because the prior conditions that prevented them from making a decision have disappeared).

This is a key concept – only an "A-1" customer will ever make a decision, regardless of what their rating was when you started the conversation or appointment.

You Can't Force It

By definition, a "B-1" customer can't make a decision.

They have one of the "ready, willing, and able" criteria to satisfy. The likeability factor is there but one of the other elements impacting their decision is missing.

The same is true of a "C-1" – with at least two of the defining criteria missing.

With a "D-1," all of the criteria for making a decision are missing.

Some people will be a "C-1" on their initial contact with you and will still be a "C-1" two years later.

You won't get a decision from everyone, and you can't force someone to change from a lower grade to an "A-1" if they really aren't ready, willing, or able to make a decision. Some people will never be able to commit to making a move.

Just be aware of the opportunities and changes in someone's personal situation that might indicate an ability to make a decision that previously was not present.

People's Situations Can Change

Just as some people will remain a "C-1" for months or even years after you meet them, others will change – sometimes between contacts with them – as their needs, requirements, and timing evolve.

While you'd like for people to change from a "C-1" to a "B-1" or even an "A-1," the change – when it occurs – won't always be in a positive direction.

Some people will move away from a decision rather than toward it.

One of the principal changes can be financial – when there is a change in employment or some type of family or medical emergency that taps into their financial resources.

Their household size can change as babies are born, adult children move back in, and divorces occur.

Also, the way that they feel about working with you or what you're showing them can change – what they liked or didn't care for previously can now be very different.

Only a few people can be an "A-1" customer at any one time – and some of your customers may never move up from their initial grade to that next higher rating.

Nevertheless, you need to be committed to monitoring all of your customers for changes in their personal and economic situations that will move them closer to (or occasionally even further away from) the time when they can make a decision with you.

6

Don't Discount The "D"s

What A "D" Rating Means

A "D" rating does not represent "discard" or "don't bother" or "don't waste your time" or "dud."

It is not a rating that is used when you can't think of anything else to use – it is not a "default" score.

It is not a rating that you give to an otherwise "A" customer who simply doesn't like you or want to work with you.

It's not a rating that you give to someone that you don't like or don't want to get to know because of your initial impressions.

While many brokers and salespeople think that a "D" customer is a total waste of their time, the fact is that some people who visit your open house or meet you truly aren't in a position to make a decision on a new home at that time – or at any time in the foreseeable or even distant future.

When I use a "D" rating, I generally figure on at least a year before someone is capable of making a decision.

A "D" Customer Is Not "Able"

With a "D" customer, this is not a case of someone just not "willing" to make a decision but rather a general inability to make a decision – even if they really would like to do so.

Mostly, we're talking about not being "able" for financial reasons to make a decision until the passage of time has allowed someone to rectify some of the issues that prevent a more timely decision.

This is different from someone who says that it will be at least a year or more before they are interested in making or considering a move ("willing").

Reasons For A "D" Rating

There are several reasons why someone might be rated a "D" – and none of them are because it's a "default" rating when nothing else is known about someone or when that person is not likeable or pleasant.

People may have credit or financial issues because of poor payment histories, large credit card balances, foreclosures, or repossessions. Perhaps they haven't established themselves in a new job or area well enough to be considered creditworthy.

They could have extremely large, unexpected medical expenses.

Their credit score may be lower than any lender will use, their household income is too low to qualify for even the most liberal of terms for the type of property they are seeking, or they may be in a negative equity situation in their current home.

However, money might not be the issue. In fact, qualifying for a loan may have nothing to do with it.

Some people are "professional lookers" — always looking but never buying. They never find anything they like because they don't intend to move.

They cannot be regarded as potentially serious buyers.

In fact, you may wonder why such people even bother to make the effort to have you show them around because they clearly have no intention of obtaining a new home.

Some of your traffic may include people who have recently purchased a home with another agent, from a homebuilder, or a home for-sale-by-owner – even if they have not closed or moved into their new residence.

They will tell you that they are "*looking for decorating ideas*" or just continuing to explore the market to "*see what else is available (out there)*" – or they may not tell you until later that they've already purchased something.

Your traffic also could include people who are going to remodel their current home – or just completed it.

Such individuals are committed to their current homes and do not foresee an immediate move. They clearly fail to have any motivation for making a decision.

There could even be other, more serious reasons or issues (such as a medical emergency or a chronic health condition of a family member) that might prevent someone from making a decision on a new home for an indefinite period of time.

Keeping It In Perspective

It's important in working with a "D" customer to remain objective – particularly about financial issues.

You may want to list their present home or help them find and buy another home, but they owe too much on their present home or just can't afford to get the type of home that will meet their needs.

In such cases, even if they would like to look for another home, this cannot outweigh the facts at hand.

You may empathize – even sympathize – with this situation or condition, but that won't help them to be able to purchase a home with you.

The financial, previous commitment, medical, credit, or other conditions that someone might have does not allow a decision for the foreseeable future.

No matter how much you might like someone or want them to have a new home, the issues prohibiting such a decision speak for themselves.

You just need to be patient until the issues resulting in the "D" rating can be addressed or resolved.

A "D" Rating Can Change

A "D" rating does not mean necessarily that this condition is permanent!

This is a very important concept.

Just because you are assigning a "D" rating to someone – for the simple reason that they are not able to make a decision – does not mean that they'll never be in a position to purchase a new home or sell their existing one. So don't throw their name away and forget about them.

It may take a year or even longer for it to change, but there is a possibility that a person currently in this position may someday be able to purchase a new home with someone – possibly you.

What if someone's condition actually does change in the next year or two?

Are you still going to be selling and listing homes in a few years? I'd like to think that you are.

When The "D" Rating Changes

So the "D" rating isn't necessarily permanent, and it can change to something that signifies a greater willingness or ability in buying a new home.

The question, then, is do you think that someone who used to be a "D" – because they were not able to qualify to purchase a new home or because they had personal or family issues that prevented even considering a decision at that time – might appreciate working with someone (such as you) who treated them with respect during that period of a year or more rather than appearing as though it was a waste of their time?

But, what if their condition does not change? What have you lost by being nice to someone and maintaining a little contact with them over the course of several months – except possibly a little time?

What does it really cost for you to be pleasant and professional to someone – even if they never acquire a home with you or ever move from their current residence?

What if they leave your area to live elsewhere or never move from their present city to yours?

What if their financial condition doesn't improve?

What if they don't decide to sell the home that they just bought with someone else and move again?

Those are definite possibilities.

On the other hand, just a little of your time to maintain contact with your "D" customers may lead to a future sale when their condition changes.

Even without a sale, you'll likely create an ambassador – and referrals are possible as well.

"D" Actually Means "D-1"

So far in this chapter, I have been talking about the "D" rating as applying to anyone who is incapable of making a decision or qualifying for financing for more than a year – for economic, family, health, or other reasons.

That's only part of the story.

You have to add in the *likeability* factor in order to have some chance of a return on your investment.

Thus, when I talk about the possibilities of a "D" customer having some value to you, I'm not talking about just anyone who is unwilling or uninterested in *ever* making a decision but someone who might eventually make a decision involving you.

I'm not suggesting that you maintain contact and stay connected with someone who can't or won't make a decision for over a year who doesn't at least like working with you.

Therefore, in this chapter, whenever I mention or talk about the "D" customers, I'm actually referring to the "*D-1*" customers.

The "D-1" is someone who has issues to overcome that will take at least a year – or more – to resolve, but they like you and what you offer well enough to want to work with you when and if that time comes.

Your "D-1" customers are people you can invest a little time in because of the possibility that a moving decision will eventually happen.

They are worth maintaining occasional contact with over time to monitor their progress and help them to feel good about you and your company.

Looking At The Bigger Picture

Other agents might not see the potential value in working with a "D" or "D-1" customer and dismiss or discount them as being unworthy of their time or energy.

They likely would not be willing to invest very much time in them or make a very meaningful presentation to them – or consider them for referrals or as potential word-of-mouth ambassadors.

In short, other real estate agents would essentially consider a "D" or "D-1" to be a waste of their time.

While they would only be looking for the more obvious sales possibilities, you understand the larger picture.

You have the ability to see and interpret the condition that prevents a person from making a decision on a new home as one that very well may be temporary.

Obviously, you would not spend time making a lengthy presentation with lesser-qualified or uninterested people at the expense of ignoring other, more qualified customers.

Nevertheless, even a brief encounter with a "D-1" customer can be polite, pleasant, and professional if you want it to be – and it will make an impression on such a customer.

Being Strategic With "D-1"s

Just think of the advantage you'll have over the other agents who weren't as professional, considerate, or kind to the "D"s or "D-1"s as you.

Remember what the potential value of the "D-1" customer is to you and your company in terms of sharing your message and kindness with others and the relative ease of maintaining contact with such customers over the course of the coming year or years – until such time as they might be able to make a decision.

Of course, some of the people who are rated a "D-1" will never move from the home they're in now or buy a new one – from you or anyone else. Their economic or personal situation may never change to the point that they are able to do so.

Nevertheless, the cost of maintaining occasional contact with your "D-1"s and monitoring if and how their situation might change over time is minimal – and quite strategic considering the potential for them eventually doing business with you.

Maintaining Appropriate Contact

Going forward from your initial meeting, you're going to have minimal contact with "D-1" customers – perhaps just once or twice a year and maybe just a brief call or email.

It won't take much of your time, but it can pay potential future dividends as you keep them involved with you until they are ready to make a purchasing decision – or you determine that it isn't likely to ever happen.

The key to maintaining effective contact with "D-1" customers is to keep it infrequent and focus on maintaining the positive, professional relationship you established during your initial meeting or conversation.

They shouldn't feel any pressure to act because both you and they recognize that they won't be doing anything about another home for many months, if at all.

A "D-1" customer won't suddenly turn into an "A-1" just because you and the customer want it to happen.

It has to run its course, but your contact with them will help you anticipate when their situation is changing to the point that they might be in a position to sell their home or buy another with you.

The Purpose Of Your Contact

One of the chief reasons for maintaining contact, albeit infrequently, with your "D-1" customers is to help insure that they remember you and your company so they will be inclined to want to do business with you if there ever comes a time when they are in a position to sell their present home or purchase their next home.

Remember also that they might be able to refer someone to you, and you want them to feel welcome to do so.

Your contact with your "D-1" customers really has two purposes: primarily, it's to keep your name in front of them (even if it is only once or twice a year), and secondarily, you need to be in a position to determine when their situation has changed to warrant a higher rating and more assertive action on your part.

Once you determine that a "D-1" customer is able to consider buying their next home, you can provide the appropriate amount of contact to help them make that decision.

7

Grading Outside The Lines

Other Types Of Traffic

So far, we've been concentrating on how you work with your conventional traffic – people that contact you in your office or open house.

You then assign a score or grade to each customer based on what you discover about their interest level in having you list their current home or in buying a new one.

When they like what you can offer them well enough to consider working with you as their agent, you add the suffix "1" to their "A," "B," "C," or "D" letter grade.

However, there are other types of traffic and contacts that you'll want to note and keep track of – to provide a more complete picture of who you talk with and to guide you in your follow-up contact.

The types of traffic that we're going to look at briefly in this chapter are important to you and your business, but usually, they will not be the ones who are making a decision to have you list their current home or help them purchase their next home.

As such, they will not be receiving any of the traditional ratings that we've been discussing so far.

Nevertheless, they can be a powerful force for you in generating positive word-of-mouth marketing (WOMM) and referrals based on their perceptions and impressions of working with you and your company.

Recording The Visit

Let anyone in these other categories, that you will be creating, learn about you and what you have to offer – and make a record of who they are. Just count these contacts separately from your regular customers.

Don't count anyone as a customer unless they actually are looking to do something for themselves.

However, if they seem genuinely interested in working with you and could be a candidate for a new home, count them as a customer and grade them accordingly.

Just don't assign a letter grade to them unless they expressly are looking for a home for themselves.

Your discovery questions are important and will make the determination about the purpose of their visit and their level of interest. This is how you'll know whether to count them in one of these other categories or as a regular customer.

The Trades

The first group of people that you want to make a note of – outside of your traditional rating system – is the one that includes anyone associated with the building trades or construction industry.

This group we will designate "TRADES."

This group does not include people like other agents or brokers, architects, designers, or decorators. They are in other groups.

Use "*trades*" to apply to people such as carpenters, electricians, roofers, plumbers, masons, siding installers, cement finishers, carpet and flooring installers, cabinet and countertop people, tile installers, painters, drywallers, landscapers, and any other building or construction tradespeople.

They may just want to learn more about what is going on in the market from your perspective – or in trying to form some type of strategic alliance or vendor relationship to provide services to you or your company.

Professionals

The next group of people that you want to make a note of is the one that includes anyone with some type of professional interest or affiliation with the real estate or construction industry.

This group we will designate "PROFESSIONALS."

Use the term "*professionals*" for architects, attorneys, interior designers, decorators, appraisers, landscape architects, model merchandisers, stagers, mortgage brokers, lenders, homebuilders, remodelers, salespeople who work for homebuilders, or other professionals who simply want to learn more about what is going on in the market from your perspective — or in trying to form a strategic alliance with you to provide services to you or your company.

Brokers

Use the term "BROKER" for any real estate agent, sales professional, or broker who visits your open house or contacts you for information about one of your listings. It's not important what title actually appears on their business card.

This category is just used to count the number of times any real estate agent (regardless of their actual title) contacts you without or prior to customers present.

It's normal for builder's new home sale representatives in your area to want to meet you, learn about your properties, and see what you're offering.

However, count builder's representatives in the "professional" category, and save the "broker" designation for anyone who potentially can produce a cooperative sale with you.

When a broker accompanies a customer, they are the "source" and the customer is graded according to their level of interest and ability to make a decision – just as if they came in from an ad, an open house sign, or your website.

In this case, count just the customer and not the broker in your traffic summary.

If a broker returns alone on the customer's behalf, count that visit as a "*returning*" visit just as if the customer had come back in with the broker or on their own.

Third-Party

The next group of people that you want to make a note of is the one that we will designate "THIRD PARTY."

"*Third-party*" applies to someone who says that they are collecting information for someone else who is not present with them (cousin, parent, grandparent, aunt or uncle, son or daughter, sibling, co-worker, friend, trustee, financial advisor, or neighbor).

They may really be doing as they say – looking for a home and collecting information for a friend or relative who is not with them.

On the other hand, this may be just an excuse that they are using to keep from revealing too much information about their own needs.

Try to collect as much detail as you can about the absent person (their name and contact information – and their relationship to the person present on their behalf) while at the same time evaluating the possible interest of the "third-party" customer who is present.

Be aware that the "third-party" person may actually be disguising their own interest. If you suspect this to be the case, you should grade the "third-party" as a regular customer with whatever information you can obtain.

Use a "C" or "C-1" rating as a good "default" starting point if you aren't sure how to grade them.

Other

The last category of people that you want to make a note of is the one that we will call "OTHER" to apply to anyone else.

This can include someone making a delivery or someone who just stops in your office or open house for directions or has general questions about the market or what you have available.

Telephone Contacts

In addition to people who stop in your office or open house, you will likely receive contact two other ways – by *telephone* and *email*.

When someone telephones for information, they may just want directions to your office or open house – having seen your phone number on a sign, billboard, or print ad. Maybe they visited your website.

They may have questions about what you have available or what you can show them – or be looking for a "mini-presentation" from you over the phone as they are trying to determine who to work with.

They may be trying to eliminate you from further consideration or keep you on their list just on the basis of what they learn during this phone call.

Obtaining Value From Calls

Do your best to obtain the caller's name and their telephone number. Answer their questions, but do your own discovery at the same time.

As you learn about the customer and their needs, write down their responses on your information card.

A great way to get a telephone number is to tell your caller that you may think of something later that you wished you would have told them or something that you would like to have asked them about to be able to serve them better – and you'd like to be able to give them a quick call to share this additional information or ask your questions.

Another way is to say that you've been having a little trouble with your phones and you'd like to have a number to call them right back if you drop the call.

You can also use caller ID, but the person calling may be using a different number than you would use to reach them on a callback – or they might have the number blocked.

You can always confirm that the number they're calling you from is a good number to use to call them back.

This gives you permission to call them as well.

If you like, you can just ask people for their telephone number – without any story or pretense.

If you aren't able to learn very much about the caller's needs on the initial call, a "C-1" is a good default rating because it assumes that they like you — and it will work until you learn enough about them to verify the rating or adjust it as necessary.

Email Inquiries

Many people will email you directly from your website.

They may ask for information about specific homes, pricing, or features — even when this information is already on your website.

Or, they may have questions that will help them decide if they want to continue getting to know you and your company.

Part of this might be just to establish the initial contact and see how you respond to the request.

You won't necessarily be able to determine enough information to give someone a score or letter grade that accurately reflects their level of interest or decision making ability — again, the "C-1" designation is a good starting point.

Starting an information card should be relatively easy.

Depending on what information your online contact form requires, you will have at a minimum of their name and email address.

You may also be collecting their address, telephone number, and information about their needs (price range, number of bedrooms and baths, approximate occupancy or listing date – and if they are interested in buying, selling, or both).

Just as with all of the special categories discussed in this chapter, count telephone or email inquiries separately from your "walk-in" traffic because they have not yet physically met with you.

8

Getting The Most From Your Traffic

Using Your Rating System

I know that you have some type of a rating system to keep track of your traffic – or will be creating one soon.

Maybe you haven't been using a formal rating system but you were just keeping track of the "good ones" in your head – or in your computer.

Perhaps you really haven't been paying that much attention to your other customers.

Possibly, you've been using a rating system for just the "good" ones and dumped the majority of your traffic in the "C" or "NR" (not rated) categories.

No matter where you have been in terms of keeping tabs on your traffic when you picked up this book and started reading it, you weren't getting the amount of impact out of a rating system that you should.

It might be a little harsh to say, but it's true.

You didn't have the maximum ability to keep track of your traffic and schedule your time to work where you could be the most effective.

You haven't been efficient.

Now all that's changed.

Now you have the modified "**A-B-C + 1**" system.

It's time to make the switch from what you have been using – or to start using my system if you've just had an informal one prior to now.

Stop Chasing After People

Now you have a very special rating system that lets you focus just on the people that like working with you instead of trying to "chase" after people that have no interest in listing or buying a home with you.

The issue with chasing after people has nothing to do with your persistence or diligence.

When you chase after people, you usually end up frustrated because you get hardly any response from them – just unanswered phone calls, unreturned voice mail messages, and unanswered email. This is because they are intentionally eluding you. They don't want to be contacted.

However, when you use the "1" suffix to denote people who like you well enough and what you can offer to consider working with you, you can avoid investing time on uninterested people.

You can "chase" people all you want, but if you can't show people something they are interested in, or they don't like your approach, you're just not going to connect with them.

You will chase them further and further away and become exhausted in the process – with no sales to show for your efforts.

Maximizing Your Effort

Rather than trying to track down people who are avoiding you because they have no real interest in a new home or in working with you, it makes sense to me for you to work with those people who have at least expressed an interest in wanting to work with you.

Doesn't this seem like a better use of your time?

The real reason you grade, rank, score, or rate your customers is so that you have a quick idea of generally where they are in the decision making process, how you and your company factor into that process, and who you need to focus on the most.

There is nothing special or magical about scoring people or in the score itself.

It's what the grade or score represents and what it tells you about someone's relative degree of readiness to make a decision on a home that counts.

People change – be ready for it. Expect it. Anticipate it. Their situations change. Their attitudes change.

Make sure their scores change as well – up or down, with a "1" added or removed.

Some people move closer to a decision, and some move further away. Some people abandon their home search entirely.

Likewise, someone who had seemed ready to make a quick decision may now be unable to do so for weeks or longer – if ever.

Some may get "caught-up" in the enthusiasm of your presentation and seem more interested in listing or in getting a home than they really are.

They may even try to convince themselves that they are more interested or closer to making a decision than actually is true.

Be Honest With Your Ratings

Don't be hasty in trying to decide which people you need to work with and which require little additional attention from you. Let the ratings work for you.

Your assessment of someone's potential to do business with you and your company should never be based on emotion. Sometimes this is hard to remember.

You really want to achieve an accurate portrayal of the quality of your traffic and formulate an effective contact strategy for working with everyone – ranging from almost daily contact for the "A-1" to infrequent contact for a "C-1" to virtually none for a "D-1."

It's easy to label or rate someone an "A" or "A-1" because it was pleasant talking with them, they were dressed well, or they seemed to share some of your same interests.

Never forget that they have to meet the established criteria. It's that simple.

Don't give someone an "A-1" rating just because you like them or because you have empathy for their situation.

Don't give it because they are "nice" people or because you believe they will buy a home with you as soon as they sell their current home.

To be an "A-1" customer, they must pass the test. They must fulfill all four criteria.

This does not mean that they are any better as a person than a "D-1" or any other customer. It just means they are ready to buy their next home now – and from you.

Remember the rating has nothing to do with their personality or value as a person. It only signifies their relative ability to make a decision.

The Race Against The Clock

There is no prize for collecting and amassing the most "A-1" customers.

This should never be your goal because you will only have one or two "A-1"s at any given time anyway.

"A-1"s in and of themselves don't pay anything. Listings can, and closed transactions do.

The only difference between an "A-1" rating and any other rating is that the "A-1" customer is ready to make a decision and capable of making one very soon. You stand a good chance of making the sale with them.

Remember that your "A-1" customers are your best potential for a sale at any given moment, and that you only have a very short amount of time to capitalize on this opportunity – days or even hours.

For planning your follow-up contact, we say that you have 3-4 weeks maximum to make a sale happen with an "A-1," but it's usually much less than that.

Actually, you may only have a day or two from when you initially meet an "A-1" to make a sale with them.

You're in competition with other brokers, builders, and homes for-sale-by-owner that also can meet this "A-1" customer's needs – and the clock is ticking.

Time is of the essence. You have to act quickly to make the sale or listing happen.

You shouldn't appear to be desperate, just diligent.

The 30-Day Buying Cycle

The 30-day buying cycle is one of convenience. It's arbitrary.

However, if an "A-1" customer actually had a buying cycle that was 30 days long when they started looking for a home, they may be at or near the end of their cycle when they contact you for the first time.

They may have essentially made up their mind on what they want and where they are going to buy it before they ever visit you.

Literally, as they walk out the door and leave your office or open house, their mind could be made up in favor of another agent, homebuilder, or home for-sale-by-owner even though they enjoyed working with you and liked what you showed them.

It could also be a case of them just not liking what you showed them or your approach – even though they are ready to make a decision.

So when you call them back a couple of days after their visit with you, they may tell you that they already bought or decided on something else.

You may not really have 30 days to work with an "A-1" customer – so plan accordingly and be prepared.

Planning For Your "A-1" Traffic

To really understand where your "A-1" customers are in their decision-making process and where you are in your follow-up contact with them, take the initiative and don't leave anything to chance.

Each morning as you start your sales day, review your notes on each "A-1" customer (the one or two that you have) so you are totally aware of what has transpired with each one and you are ready to make the sale.

It doesn't matter that you just looked at those cards and notes the day before, and the day before that. Look at them again.

Look at what still needs to happen for your "A-1"s to be able to say "yes" to your final closing question.

Then make certain that all planned contact with each "A-1" customer is being accomplished and that no opportunities for contact are overlooked or lost.

You won't necessarily be contacting each "A-1" customer every single day, but you need to be aware of what you have done and what remains to be done with each one so you can plan and execute your next contact.

Be ready for a phone call or email from them or a surprise, impromptu, drop-in visit.

Just make sure that there are no surprises or missed opportunities and that you can take full advantage of each contact.

Managing Your Other Traffic

After you review your "A-1" customers each day, turn next to reviewing and monitoring your "B-1" and your

"C-1" customers. Remember, future "A-1" customers – and sales and listings – will come from here.

Depending on how many "B-1" customers you have, plan on reviewing 25% or so each day so that you've reviewed all of them within 3-4 days. Then start over again.

Take a few more days to review all of your "C-1"s and then repeat.

If you have a relatively small amount of "B-1" and "C-1" customers on file and you have the time to do so, you can review all of them or as many as you like each day.

As you have time, check your "D-1" customers as well.

Start with your "B-1" and "C-1" customers who seem to have the highest probability of moving up to the next rank and strategize your follow-up contact to identify how to make that happen.

You have rated your "B" and "C" customers (without using the suffix "1") because they expressed little or no interest in working with you, so you won't schedule any regular contact with them.

However, as you are up-to-date with all of your other contacts, occasionally call a "B" or "C" customer to check on their search for a home. Remember people are subject to change in both needs and life situations.

You could learn information about them that could cause you to re-evaluate their status.

The Real Pay-Off

To maximize the results from using this rating system that I have given you, keep in mind that it is strictly objective, and as such will give you an unbiased profile of the relative strength of your traffic – individually and collectively.

It is based on the “ready, willing, and able” test plus whether they “like” you and think you can help them.

It has no bearing on anyone’s personality, how well you like them, or what you think of someone as a person.

You may “hit it off” with someone because you have similar personalities or enjoy common interests and are able to establish a great rapport with them.

Still, you should only rate them according to their ability to make a decision and not on how well you like them.

Conversely, if you do not relate to someone on a personal level, this is no reason to give them anything less than your highest rating – if they actually are ready to acquire a home and meet the test.

It’s the criteria that matter and nothing else.

This rating system takes the personal element out of the scoring — as long as you do a good job of discovery.

All it takes to rate someone's level of interest and ability to make a purchasing or listing decision is for you to determine the answers to four very simple questions: are they *ready* to make a decision, are they *willing* to make a decision, are they *able* to make a decision, and do they *like* you well enough to work with you?

Your ability to get answers to those questions will directly impact how effective and efficient you are in your real estate business.

You'll be able to concentrate and focus on the people with the highest ratings and de-emphasize those without the "1" rating.

The higher the rating, the closer you are to a sale or listing.

It *is* that simple.

Steve Hoffacker

Steve Hoffacker, CAPS, MCSP, MIRM, is principal of Hoffacker Associates LLC, a sales training (new home sales, universal design, and aging-in-place) and coaching company based in West Palm Beach, Florida.

Steve is an award-winning, internationally-recognized and experienced new home salesperson and sales trainer, as well as a universal design/aging-in-place safety and accessibility sales trainer and instructor.

For more than 30 years, he has helped homebuilders, new home salespeople, contractors and remodelers, new home marketers, designers, architects, occupational therapists, and other professionals to be more visible, competitive, profitable, and effective – and to really enjoy themselves as they pursue their business and create wonderful customer experiences.

Steve wants you and your company to be successful and has created this guide (and many others) to help make that happen.

This book will be a great resource to help you take your business to another level and outpace the competition.

Use these strategies and concepts for your professional success.

www.ingramcontent.com/pod-product-compliance
Lightning Source LLC
LaVergne TN
LVHW010929110826
845149LV00013B/2527

* 9 7 8 0 9 8 4 3 5 2 4 1 8 *